Time and Tide

Kerri Diplock

BookLeaf Publishing

Presentation by *BookLeaf Publishing*

Web: www.bookleafpub.com

E-mail: info@bookleafpub.com

ISBN: 9789357211772

First edition 2023

DEDICATION

To my Mother who has forever been my strongest foundation and admirer

To my Dad who chose to be,

There once was a man with a daughter

A brunette, and he said that she oughta

Publish her book

To stop being a sook

And remember everything that he taught her.

And my husband and children - you always encourage my strengths.

ACKNOWLEDGEMENT

Foremost, I have to thank my Mum for mostly everything. My first love, advocate, confidant.... friend. Her days were never burdened by my troubles. She has always encouraged my creativity and gave me the confidence to be myself. Weighted by her own life, she gave us all she could and more. I can never express the love I have for her and how much her sacrifice has allowed me to have the life I love.
My Dad, Eddie, was the most colourful character you'd meet. An Aussie bloke through and through, full of yarns and experience. Dad taught me to stop and think and question my world. To ask questions without speaking, to belong to a place where the sheep don't herd. And he listened. He always listened. He was the only one that could understand my odd questions without becoming frustrated by my ignorance. But I soon learnt that if I asked a stupid question, I'd get a stupid answer!
Dennis - my Dad's best friend and too educated for the people he lived amongst. A humble helper, and never one to judge ability or status. He always leant an educated ear to help with school and life's issues. My unofficial second

Dad told me to live life "Stupid Simple" and to this day I heed his advice. I kin thee Dennis. My brother and sister have both been great sources for understanding myself, prompting behaviour both favourable and regretful, creating great emotion and motivation to write. I consider myself a lucky big sister.

I have my husband and children to thank for making this book happen. All four of them have constantly encouraged my writing and want to see me succeed. Their faith in me and love goes unmatched and I will forever smile because of them.

Thank you to everyone who has ever read my work and felt an emotion or a tear work its way to your cheek because you could feel your own belonging within my words. You make my writing more than appreciated.

PREFACE

Time and Tide waits for no man. That's what my Dad would often say. He's not been earthside for four years now, but he still says it. Every time I'm running late, every time a deadline is nigh, every time I celebrate a birthday.... Time and tide. This year I acknowledge that I have lived for forty years. This year I inevitably reminisce my time and ponder how long they'll continue to say my name when I'm only photographs and memories. This book is for my children. It is for my children's children. These words capture the complexity of my simple, ordinary life and guarantees me an identity that will outlive my forebears. Forty years old is the perfect time to begin something I've always wanted to do.

My Rainbow

Red is for love
When all you feel is pain.
Orange is for sunshine
To clear away the rain.
Yellow is for friendship
To mend a broken trust.
Green is for new life
To relieve a drought's dust.
Blue is for happiness
To wipe those tears away.
Indigo is for my love
So you'll know I'm there each day.
Violet is all the love
To me, each day, you give.
My rainbow is all of these feelings
But you are the one who helps them live.

A Special Friendship

Once I was so tiny
Too small for this world.
Your loving arms embraced me,
Your charming baby girl.

Months had passed since then
But still your pride and joy,
I felt your love, so big it was,
Your presence I enjoyed.

When I hurt or was upset
On your shoulder I'd bury my head.
My wet tears flowed all over you
'Let it all out' you had said.

I loved the games we played together
I thought those days would never end.
We'd cheer and smile forever -
You were my best friend.

Although the years have passed
And things have changed since then.
I still enjoy our times together,
You're still my very best friend.

Mummy

There's a woman in my life,
I must confess,
Who loves me more
Than I can guess.

She shows a love
That is so rare.
A love that shows me
That she cares.

She makes me feel happy
In every way
And she shows me she loves me
Every day.

I wonder if she knows it
One way or another
That nothing beats the true love
Of my mother!

As Deaf as Dumb

She calls to you
But you won't hear her.
She cries to you in pain.
Her anxiety to reach you -
Neverending, unexpressed.
But you won't hear her.

Her calls are loud and understood
But you won't hear her.
She gets louder and clearer
With every painful cry.
She only wants to tell you
But you won't hear her.

Her body is frustrated
But you won't hear her.
Every aching, communicating part of
Her body and soul becomes crushed
And she goes quietly -
All because you won't hear her.

A Sudden Burning Blackness

The night burns long into the night
Fire and fear are full of fright.
She pulls the gun to her head
And nothing more can be heard or said.
Her body lay in a pile of lies
Because of those whores she had to die.
The night is old, but she is young
Her colding heart destroys the sun.
Her sweet, thick blood is shared to all
The memories now stand so tall.
Her ugly veins yield blood no more.
Her shattered brain asks 'What for?'
She withers under pale moonlight.
She will not know if she was right.
A life is taken without a thought
But no one will care, their hearts are bought.
The innocent mind using a loaded gun.
'The whore deserved it' says everyone.
She searched so long to leave her life so damned
Until tonight, when it was placed in her hand.
The innocence and blame she endures no more
Because her soul and flesh are neatly torn.
She will not know she had no right
But the day was long and the night.
The gun was best - her only friend.

She chose this burning night to have it end.
And the trees tell a silent tale of fear and fright
That she suffered, this long burning night.

To My Friend

If you wake and find no sun
And it seems to fall on everyone
I will find your sunshine.

If your eyes create a lake
And from reality you cannot wake
I will find a dream for you.

If a storm should come your way
And cloud the light in your day
I will find the calm.

If you cry tears of joy and pride
And life takes you on an adventurous ride
I will be your friend.

'Cause when I wake and find no sun
And all my rivers start to run
When my storms cloud out my light
And my tears show of my happy life
You're always there to light my day
And help me dream in every way
You always seem to find the calm
And help to find my life's charms.

Different Similarities

I look at you and see an innocent youth
Matured by all of your supposed guilt.
You are his daughter, his flesh and blood.
There's no escape.

Your features are strong, exact almost to his
Yet they are weak in comparison.
You will grow and be like him always
There's no escape.

Your thoughts my child, are wild and vivid
Yet they are logical and sensitive to you both.
You cannot escape these dreams my girl
There's no escape.

Your love for him is so strong, so deep
Yet it is paper thin, almost transparent.
You think your love in unrequited
There's no escape.

I can see from your image most times you hurt
Yet you always seem to smile.
Pain seems like a wonderful thing to you, but
There's no escape.

And when I look at you now, as I will towards death
I know what it is you feel.
You're still my innocent little girl, you're image is truthful because
There's no escape from the truth of a mirror's reflection.

Sister

I only wish that you could see
The happiness you have given me
I cherish you more than you think I do
My sun wouldn't shine without you.
You're everything Santa and I had planned
There's no one like you in this land
I treasure our memories - they're gold to me
They remind me of the way things used to be.
But things do change and even you
Have changed my way of life, it's true
I spent three years waiting for you to come
And when you arrived, my life begun.
So when things go wrong for you
I promise to be there to help you through
I'll be your sun, I'll guide your way
So you can smile yet another day.

Cleansing the Land

The cicadas sing the silence
And the storm birds sing their song
The sky is filled with promise
The dry has been too long.
The blackened sky starts to rumble
The birds at once take wing
The cool air starts to repair
All the heat and suffering.
The earth stands still a moment
The trees hold their branches still
The wind forgets its purpose
And the dams pray for their fill.
Then the wind puppeteers the trees
It brings a heavenly smell
The dry will be forgotten tomorrow
When they measure how much had fell.
Rain falls down in bucketloads
Cleansing all below
Nurturing all that was forgot
All those weeks and months ago.
Water settles deep into the earth
And brings a life anew
Then the sun comes out to see
Answered prayers for me and you.

Little Brother, Call for me

Little brother, call for me
Are you hungry, do you want sleep?
Little brother, call for me
You hide and I will seek.
Little brother, call for me
I can read you that book.
Little brother, call for me
You lost your toy? I'll look.
Little brother, call for me
I can tie your shoes.
Little brother, call for me
We'll make some giblet soup.
Little brother, call for me
I'll get you safe to school.
Little brother, call for me
Which kid has picked on you?
Little brother, call for me
I can help you with your work.
Little brother, call for me
I'll chase the monsters that lurk.
Little brother, call for me
I feel those feelings too.
Little brother, call for me
I need someone too.
Little brother, call for me

I've started a new life.
Little brother, call for me
I'll help you when in strife.
Little brother, call for me
Meet your small nephew.
Little brother, call for me
I'll always make time for you.
Little brother, call for me
I'll guide you best I can.
Little brother, call for me
When did you become a man?
Little brother, call for me
You have a little niece.
Little brother, call for me
I hope that you find peace.
Little brother, call for me
Don't be silly, we all cry.
Little brother, call for me
Of course I'll come on by.
Little brother, call for me
I'm sorry to move away.
Little brother, call for me
I'll see you soon one day.
Little brother, call for me
How's life been treating you?
Little brother, call for me
I have exciting news.
Little brother, call for me
Your youngest niece is here.

Little brother, call for me
I wish that you were here.
Little brother, call for me
Tell Dad I'm on my way.
Little brother, call for me
Dad will be OK.
Little brother, call for me
It hurts to be so far away.
Little brother, call for me
We're moving home today.
Little brother, call for me
I'm driving in right now.
Little brother, call for me
We'll all get through this somehow.
Little brother, call for me
Dad's left us through the night,
My little brother, called for me
To make sure I was alright.
Little brother, call for me
I heard you'll be a Dad.
Little brother, call for me
I'm so very glad.
Little brother, call for me
It's OK, one step after another.
Little brother, call for me
I'm always here little brother.
Little brother, call for me
I heard you have a daughter!
Little brother, call for me

I don't phone as much as I oughta.
Little brother, call for me
I'll tell you what I can.
Little brother, call for me
You are an awesome Dad.
Little brother, call for me
I'm just a call away.
Little brother, call for me
I hope that you're OK?
Little brother, call for me
I'm always by my phone.
Little brother, call for me
I never want you to feel alone.

Nanny's little girl

Mum, I closed my eyes
And I could see
Someone smiling
At the bride-to-be.
Her smile was pure
Like heaven above
And through my thoughts
She sent her love.
I felt her presence
So strong, so true
"Nanny?" I said
"Is that really you?"
She continued to smile
And then I knew
She had come to me
Just for you.
She was just as beautiful
As I had ever known
And her smile kept widening
Thinking of how you'd grown.
Her daughter, her girl
My friend, my mum.
We smiled at each other
As I knew why she'd come.
Her pride outshone the stars

As we stood silently together.
I know that she is happy
Now and forever.
She seemed at ease
And happy to know
That you will again dress in white
And have your children let you go.
Mum, no words were spoken
But I know what she said
And she is proud to know
That you will soon be wed.
She may not zip up
Your beautiful gown
Or hold your skirt
From off the ground.
She may not toast to you
But do not dismay
Because Nanny told me
She will be there on your special day.
The soft breeze on your cheek,
The tear in your eye,
The whisper you hear,
The glow in the sky.
She will stand with you,
Like no other
For she still feels
So much love for my mother.

For my Children

When our worlds are far apart
And you can't feel the warmth of my heart.
Look to the moon and know that, too
I look to the moon when I think of you.
Although we may share the night alone
Just know that soon I will be home.

The Purest of Love

Oh how one day I hope you'll feel this love
I pray you'll know it too.
It lives in every breath you take
And changes all you knew.

The first flutter as they move within
When you hear their beating heart.
When your body changes just for them
This love begins to start.

Before you meet them one by one
You dreamt what love would be.
But until you see their tiny face
You didn't know what love would mean.

You study their whole body
Seeing all that you've become.
In the instant that you meet them
You're now someone's Dad or Mum.

Women are turned into Mums.
Men proudly become Dads.
Your lives have changed in an instant
And you forget all that you have had.

You no longer live for what you want
But you do everything you need.
To give your child all that you have
Plus more than you've ever been.

The purest of loves hurt the most
And you will get your fill
Of happiness, doubt, pain and worry
And you'll wish that time stood still.

From their first bath to becoming adults
You can't begin to know
How your parents love has felt it all
And will forever continue to grow.

You'll cry when you are happy
You'll laugh when you are mad.
You'll make mistakes and learn with them -
The purest love you've had.

And as time moves forward, the years go by
And memories are all protected by the past.
Your Mum and Dad will always keep their love
for their children
Nestled gently within their hearts.

FND's Puppet

There's a problem with my circuitry
That assuming eyes won't see.
It's all in your head. You are faking it.
It's just anxiety.
Round and round the medical-go-round
In different states I've been.
Tested. Prodded. Old world knowledge.
They all haven't been able to see.
In silence I have protested,
Knowing it can't be me.
I am not a person to feign my health,
Why couldn't anyone believe?
I'm tired, my child,
I can't come over my friend.
I'm in pain, my love.
There seems to be no end.
After years of professional opinion,
I began to believe their ignorance.
Maybe I had focused too much on what I feel
And had become a medical hindrance.
But a new feeling would arrive,
A new normal in pain and tolerance.
I knew deep down it shouldn't be so
But felt outnumbered by their arrogance.
My arms will shake and tremble

My neck will twist, my limbs will writhe.
I will cry and look scared
As I try to control my mind.
You will see me at my worst
And will assume I have control
You'll think I want attention
And I am weak, that's how I roll.
But what you don't see or hear
Is how I push myself every day
To be the mother my children need
And the wife he married that day.
To do the chores you consider small
Is hard for me at best.
My normal societal roles
Send me to bed for days of rest.
My body aches and yearns for quiet
My brain can't get the signal right.
For years and years I've endured this
For years my body and brain have been at fight.
I tossed and turned during the night
Today my hands are shaking.
My jaw is making funny faces
But I'm at home - I am not faking.
I breathe steady to calm my senses
But the storm has already begun.
I lose my speech, control of me
And know the next few hours will not be fun.
My children are scared to see me,
What is wrong with Mum?

I am not their mother when
Another seizure is about to come.
Don't tell me that it's all stress.
Please don't tell me how I feel.
Please don't tell me that my MRI is clear
So it can't possibly be real.
I don't know when or how
My wiring went wrong.
But I have finally found people like me
And I know I will be strong.
For, FND won't define me
But for now it will calm my fears.
As I have tried to understand my body
For many many years.
Please don't put me into a box
And think I'm just crazy.
I have struggles, I am human
But please, let the whole world know about
FND.

To My Brother from My Other Mother

The wind blew strong today
The time was 1:03.
The leaves and bark rolled upon the grass
And the bushes curtsied to the trees.

Leaves and flowers fell from high -
Nature's confetti in the air.
Then settled gently down to rest
On an emerald bed, with care.

This eddy came from nowhere,
But it was hard and fast.
It felled the leaves from their place
And removed them from their past.

The hairs on my neck prickled
As the cool air passed over my skin.
And in that moment something unseen
Whispered loved memories of him.

In a flash I saw his face again
Then I heard his voice.
I saw him laugh so hard once more
Like he used to with the boys.

I saw the night I met him
When he asked me to be his wife.
I saw all of the memories we'd shared
In that snippet of his life.

I saw the smiles, the sleeping face,
The disgruntled so and so.
I saw the trust in the corner of his smile
That only true friends and family would know.

I saw him let his hair down,
I saw him work hard.
I saw him love and respect
Everyone in his backyard.

I remembered how he'd believe in me
When I had come undone.
I remembered the pride he'd truly had
As an uncle of two plus our son.

I remembered in that moment
The kind of love he had
For each and every one of us
And I tried hard not to be sad.

For I know that he is still here
Like the leaves upon the grass.
He's resting gently upon the earth
Where he will forever last.

Dad's Dream

I dreamt of you last night
And saw your smile again
You grinned from ear-to-ear
Like you always did back then.
I whispered 'Happy Birthday Dad'
As I leaned in for a kiss,
And felt that love flood back again,
Inside the hugs we have missed.
You leaned back into your chair
And we chatted the hours away.
I told you about the kids
And you asked if everything's been ok.
It only felt like minutes had passed
When you said you couldn't stay.
You said, 'Love ya, Doy, gotta go'
As I whispered 'Happy Birthday'.

The Silent Storm Within

Storm brewing
Dark and colourful
Rumbling deep without a sound.
Everyone can see it
But which direction do I look?
I feel the vibrations
Confused by what they say.
Not sure whether to play in the rain
Or find solace in shelter.
But why do I believe when
I don't see the sounds?
I don't see the colours.
Has the storm begun and when will it end?
I find no comfort in your reassurance
For you do not know how big the storm is.
You see it.
I feel it.
It is me.
It is all around and it twists about in my soul.
Beautiful colours as dark as my eyes and voice show.
Wanting to turn into rainbows but too immature for a future known.
Time works deeper into the eye
And I find myself trapped

Waiting for a window.
I know I have become it, and yearn to be beneath it.
Would you take me by the hand?
Hold me, help me, show me.
I have lost all and all that seems to remain
Is a bitter shell, beaten down by the chaos of the dark.
I see the rainbow... I coax it to be confident.
But alas, it is whisked up high and blown off course.
It will come.
It will end.
It must stop.
Let it out.
Show the colours.
Unmask the layers anew.
Blue shall arise and yellow and red will follow.
Grey will always watch and cower in the background
As long as blue explodes.

A night in the life of a Mum

It is now 10PM
The day has now passed,
The children are sleeping
In their beds at long last.

They sigh with contentment
And stretch with remiss,
As Mummy leans in
And gives each a kiss.

She finds her way through to the loungeroom
And yawns,
As the housework will now
Have to wait 'til the morn.

She tidies the toys
Leaves the hallway light bright,
As she makes for the shower
Then checks the scales are still right.

She turns down her bed
Checks the time, and it says,
You've gone to bed
Too late again!

She snuggles deep into the sheets
And feels her aches ease away,
Her mind now fills with a cobweb of chores
That she's remembered to do another day.

The house is so silent
But too loud to sleep,
As she mentally prepares
Diary entries to keep.

The neighbours' dogs bark
The trees squeak on the fence.
Mummy's finally finding
Her tired sleep sense.

"Waaah" through the monitor
The baby awakes,
But I just fell asleep?!
For goodness sake!

She stumbles with eyes closed
To the wee cot.
Hello my dear. I was asleep.
Had u forgot?

Let Mummy hold you and feed you
And rock you back to sleep,
Then back to her bed
Hurriedly, she creeps.

Ah, that place in bed is found again
And she falls into her dreams so sweet.
What? Why is the light on?
And I can hear hurried steps of little feet?

Mummy, I had a bad dream!
Can I please sleep with you?
Of course you can my little one,
Climb up and we'll cuddle too.

Mummy falls into her dreams again
Keeping nightmares from coming in.
Maybe now she'll get some rest,
Maybe now she'll have a win.

Pitter patter. Click. Bright light.
Ok, it's your turn now.
Mummy I'm sorry, I've wet my bed
Oh really, sweetheart. How?!

Come with me, we'll change your clothes
And set your bed just right.
So you can go back to dreaming
And sleep 'til the morning light.

Stumble. Lego. Expletive.
Mummy's bed is teasing her.
She needs a good night's sleep

To get through tomorrow's work.

Mummy gets to dream again
But with an elbow in her ear,
And wakes as the sun pierces the cracks through the blinds.....
Is that the baby she can hear?

Ok I'm coming, what a good girl!
You slept all night for Mum!
Please sleep a few more hours,
I don't think I'm quite done.

Fist pump! Silent scream!
Jump onto the bed.
Morning my love, says Daddy
As he lifts a foot out of his head.

Did bubby only then just wake?
Gee, she slept so well!
I didn't hear her all night long,
Only the neighbour's dogs from hell.

Yes she did sleep well, Mummy agrees
But I'm so very tired.
But the kids have been asleep all night
Why are you so wired?

Bub slept a good nine hours last night,

Your seven should have made you well rested?
Mummy ends the conversation here...
Mummy's kindness is being tested!

He Cancer-vive in our memories

Medicines and beanies,
Shuffling feet.
Nurses and carers,
Hospital sheets.

Bedrest from weakness
But your spirit stayed bright,
I saw in your eyes
How much you needed to fight.

Withering arms
Where muscles once grew.
You were the strongest man
That I ever knew.

As you waltzed with the devil
I came to see
Just how special
You were to me.

For thirty odd years
You were the light in my sun.
My first hero.
My number one.

You gave me everything you could
So much more than you had.
You were more than a father,
You gave me a Dad.

I remember your stories,
Your knowledge, your grin.
You helped me learn from my losses
And celebrated my wins.

You explained all the mysteries
And helped me understand
All the world around me,
You always held my hand.

You understood my weaknesses
And taught me to be strong.
To be humble when I was right
And to acknowledge when I was wrong.

'Tis better to be thought a fool
Than open your mouth and prove it.
To give the benefit of the doubt
And to let karma always sort it.

Dad, thank you for everything you gave
For every way you showed me.
Thank you for being the father

That you didn't have to be.

So roll up your sleeves,
Take off your hat.
Wipe the sweat from your brow
And leave your boots on the mat.

Your hard work is finished,
The kettle is on,
It's time for a break,
Leave nothing for 'ron.

Rest well and go easy,
No reason to wait.
We love you so much, Dad,
Catch you later mate.

Ode to Ed

Four long years without you
But I still feel you here.
You are the sun that warms at dawn,
You are the memory in my tears.
You are the calm of the morn,
You are the smell of rain.
You are the voice when I need to talk....
Forever you will remain.
The evening star shines brighter now
And the moon now lights my night.
I close my eyes and see your face
And you tell me all is right.
I know you wouldn't wish for me
To remember and be sad
So today I thank your chosen gods
For giving me my Dad.

Time and Tide

She slowly let her eyes close
As she surrendered to Nature's song.
Her furrowed brow relaxed and smoothed
As she recalled those years now gone.
A simple smile hid in the corner
Of her pursed lips and greying eyes.
The sun, the wind, the birds, her heart
Kept her weakened mind alive.
Nature's song distracted her,
Her body and mind were one.
Her heart kept the rhythm
While her mind played nostalgia's drum.
For every beat her heart did keep,
Yesterday sang the words
To the tune that was her memories,
Her life, their Mum, her world.
Gumtrees and mulberries
Horses, frogs and laughter
Music, mystery, the untouched earth
Her happy forever after.
She knew this song that nature played
Her hands relaxed their grasp.
Her body and mind were flooded with
All of the memories of her past.
She dredged about the muddied earth,

In gumboots and red cap,
She ushered all the chooks and dogs
And terrorised the cat.
She hummed along to the pain and happiness
She lived those years ago
Taking comfort in a life well lived
That many couldn't know.
A dark haired girl, with smiles and wonder
A soul who wanted more.
A little girl that needed adventure
And nature to explore.
She felt that connection to her world
That others would deny
And she sought the truth inside her,
To steer through the darkest times.
Nature's song kept playing
She watched a little girl grow strong
The lyrics could only be heard
By the one that hummed along.
A daughter, a sister, a girlfriend.
The girl then became a Mum.
Nostalgia cheered along this girl
With the beating of her heart's drum.
Her husband and their wedding day,
Her children and every birth.
Their successes and their losses,
Each all shared their worth.
As Nature's song played out it's tune,
She fondly remembered how,

Her life was more than she had known
And she knew her time was now.
Nostalgia paused the certain drum,
Her heart slowed, but her mind
Found the place she chose to end the song
Somewhere warm and loved and kind.
She felt comfort in this place,
Of beauty and of heart,
Her family held her lifeless hands
When she chose the time to part.
Nature's song had finished,
Ears of eternity had heard.
Her heart and mind had completed all
Without ever sharing a word.
Tears of passion and of love
Fell in floods of pain,
But they felt comfort in knowing that forever,
She would be dancing in the rain.

www.ingramcontent.com/pod-product-compliance
Lightning Source LLC
Chambersburg PA
CBHW051739130826
49812CB00033B/932
* 9 7 8 9 3 5 7 2 1 1 7 7 2 *